A
Little Book of
Scottish
V E R S E

Selected by David Ross

With illustrations from the
National Gallery of Scotland

Appletree Press

CONTENTS

BONNY GEORGE
CAMPBELL

High upon Hielands,
And laigh upon Tay,
Bonny George Campbell
Rade out on a day:
Saddled and bridled,
And gallant to see,
Hame cam' his gude horse,
But never cam' he.

Down ran his auld mither,
Greetin' fu' sair;
Out ran his bonny bride,
Reaving her hair.
"My meadow lies green
And my corn is unshorn,
My barn is to bigg,
And my babe is unborn."

Saddled and bridled
And booted rade he;
A plume in his helmet,
A sword at his knee;
But toom cam' his saddle,
A' bluidy to see,
O hame cam' his gude horse,
But never cam' he!

Anonymous

A Man's a Man for A' That

Is there for honest poverty
That hings his head, and a' that?
The coward slave, we pass him by –
We dare be poor, for a' that!
For a' that, and a' that!
Our toils obscure, and a' that.
The rank is but the guinea's stamp,
The man's the gowd, for a' that.

What though on hamely fare we dine,
Wear hodden grey and a' that?
Gie fools their silks, and knaves their wine –
A man's a man for a' that.
For a' that and a' that.
Their tinsel show, and a' that,
The honest man, though e'er sae poor,
Is king o' men for a' that

Then let us pray that come it may
(As come it will for a' that)
That Sense and Worth o'er a' the earth
Shall bear the gree and a' that!
For a' that, and a' that
It's comin yet, for a' that
That man to man, the world o'er,
Shall brothers be for a' that.

Robert Burns
(1759–1796)

A Rondel of Love

Lo! what it is to love,
Learn ye, that list to prove
Be me, I say, that no ways may
The ground of grief remove,
But still decay, both nicht and day:
Lo! what it is to love.

Love is ane fervent fire,
Kindlit withiut desire:
Short pleasure, lang displeasure;
Repentance is the hire:
Ane poor treasure without measure:
Love is ane fervent fire.

To love and to be wise,
To rage with good advice,
Now thus, now than, so goes the game.
Incertain is the dice.
There is no man, I say, that can
Both love and to be wise.

Flee always from the snare;
Learn at me to beware;
It is ane pain and double train
Of endless woe and care;
For to refrain that danger plain,
Flee always from the snare.

Alexander Scott
(Fl. 1547-1584)

11

To S. R. Crockett

Blows the wind today, and the sun and the rain are
    flying,
Blows the wind on the moors today and now,
Where about the graves of the martyrs the whaups
    are crying,
My heart remembers now!

Grey recumbent tombs of the dead in desert places,
Standing stones on the vacant wine-red moor,
Hills of sheep, and the howes of the silent vanished
    races,
And winds, austere and pure.

Be it granted me to behold you again in dying,
Hills of home! and to hear again the call;
Hear about the graves of the martyrs the peewees
    crying,
And hear no more at all.

Robert Louis Stevenson
(1850–1894)

The Return

(A Piper's Vaunting)

Och hey! for the splendour of tartans!
And hey for the dirk and the targe!
The race that was hard as the Spartans
Shall return again to the charge:

Shall come back again to the heather,
Like eagles, with beak and with claws
To take and to scatter for ever
The Sasunnach thieves and their laws.

Och, then, for the bonnet and feather!
The pipe and its vaunting clear:
Och, then, for the glens and the heather!
And all that the Gael holds dear.

Pittendrigh Macgillivray
(1856–1938)

THE CANADIAN BOAT SONG

Fair these broad meads – these hoary woods are grand;
But we are exiles from our fathers' land.

Listen to me, as when ye heard our father
Sing long ago the song of other shores –
Listen to me, and then in chorus gather
All your deep voices, as ye pull your oars.

From the lone sheiling of the misty island
Mountains divide us, and a waste of seas –
Yet still the blood is true, and the heart is Highland,
And we in dreams behold the Hebrides.

We ne'er shall tread the fancy-haunted valley,
Where 'tween the dark hills creeps the small, clear
        stream,
In arms around the patriarch banner rally,
Nor see the moon on royal tombstones gleam.

When the bold kindred, in the time long vanish'd,
Conquer'd the soil and fortified the keep –
No seer foretold the children would be banish'd,
That a degenerate lord might boast his sheep.

Come foreign rage – let Discord burst in slaughter!
O then for clansmen true, and stern claymore –
The hearts that would have given their blood like water
Beat heavily beyond the Atlantic roar.

Anonymous

The Jolly Beggars

To a Haggis

Fair fa' your honest, sonsie face,
Great chieftain o' the puddin'-race!
Aboon them a' ye tak your place,
Painch, tripe or thairm:
Weel are ye worthy of a grace
As lang's my arm.

The groaning trencher there ye fill,
Your hurdies like a distant hill,
Your pin wad help to mend a mill
In time o' need.
While thro' your pores the dews distil,
Like amber bead.

His knife see rustic Labour dight,
An, cut you up wi' ready slight;
Trenching your gushing entrails bright
Like ony ditch;
And then, O what a glorious sight,
Warm-reekin', rich!

Ye Pow'rs, wha mak mankind your care,
Aud dish them out their bill o' fare,
Auld Scotland wants nae skinking ware
That jaups in luggies;
But, if ye want her gratefu' prayer,
Gie her a haggis!

Robert Burns
(1759–1796)

19

O WALY, WALY

O waly, waly up the bank,
And waly, waly down the brae,
And waly, waly by yon burnside
Where I and my love wont to gae.

I leaned my back against an aik,
I thought it was a trusty tree;
But first it bow'd and syne it brak:
Sae my true love did lichtly me.

O waly, waly, but love is bonny
A little time while it is new;
But when 'tis auld, it waxeth cauld
And fades awa' like morning dew.

O wherefore should I busk my head?
O wherefore should I kame my hair?
For my true love has me forsook,
And says he'll never lo'e me mair.

And O! If my young babe were born,
And set upon the nurse's knee,
And I myself were dead and gane,
And the green grass growing over me.

Anonymous

THE TWA CORBIES

As I was walking all alane,
I heard twa corbies makin' a mane,
The t'ane unto the t'ither did say,
"Where sall we gang and dine the day?"

"In ahint yon auld fail-dyke
I wot there lies a new-slain knight;
And naebody kens that he lies there
But his hawk, and his hound, and his lady fair.

"His hound is to the hunting gane,
His hawk to fetch the wild-fowl hame;
His lady has ta'en another mate,
So we may mak our dinner sweet.

"Ye'll sit on his white house-bane,
And I'll pick out his bonny blue een,
Wi' ae lock o' his gowden hair,
We'll theek our nest when it grows bare.

"Mony a ane for him maks mane,
But none sall ken where he is gane;
O'er his white banes when they are bare,
The wind sall blaw for evermair."

Anonymous

Like the Idalian queen,
Her neck about her eyne,
With neck and breasts' ripe apples to be seen,
At first glance of the morn,
In Cyprus' gardens gathering those fair flow'rs
Which of her blood were born,
I saw, but fainting saw, my paramours.
The Graces naked danc'd about the place,
The winds and trees amaz'd
With silence on her gaz'd;
The flow'rs did smile, like those upon her face,
And as their aspen stalks those fingers band,
That she might read my case,
A hyacinth I wish'd me in her hand.

William Drummond of Hawthornden
(1585–1649)

The Highlands Swelling Blue

He who first met the Highlands swelling blue
Will love each peak that shows a kindred hue,
Hail in each crag a friend's familiar face,
And clasp the mountain in his mind's embrace.
Long have I roamed through lands which are not mine,
Adored the Alp and loved the Apennine,
Revered Parnassus and beheld the steep
Jove's Ida and Olympus crown the deep.
But t'was not all long ages' lore, nor all
Their nature held me in their thrilling thrall;
The infant rapture still survived the boy,
And Loch-na-gar with Ida look'd o'er Troy.
Mix'd Celtic memories with Phrygian mount,
And Highland linns with Castalie's clear fount.
Forgive me, Homer's universal shade,
Forgive me, Phoebus, that my fancy stray'd;
The north and nature taught me to adore
Your scenes sublime, from those beloved before.

George Gordon, Lord Byron
(1788–1824)

GLASGOW

(Extract)

City! I am true son of thine;
Ne'er dwelt I where great mornings shine
Around the bleating pens;
Ne'er by the rivulets I strayed,
And ne'er upon my childhood weighed
The silence of the glens.
Instead of shores where ocean beats,
I hear the ebb and flow of streets.

Draw thy fierce streams of blinding ore,
Smite on a thousand anvils, roar
Down to the harbour-bars;
Smoulder in smoky sunsets, flare
On rainy night, with street and square
Lie empty to the stars.
From terrace proud to alley base
I know thee as my mother's face.

When sunset bathes thee in his gold,
In wreaths of bronze thy sides are rolled,
Thy smoke is dusky fire;
And, from the glory round thee poured,
A sunbeam like an angel's sword
Shivers upon a spire.
Thus have I watched thee, Terror! Dream!
While the blue Night crept up the stream.

Alexander Thomson
(1830–1867)

MY LUVE IS LIKE A RED,
RED ROSE

O, my luve's like a red, red rose,
That's newly sprung in June,
O, my luve's like the melodie
That's sweetly played in tune.

As fair art thou, my bonnie lass,
So deep in luve am I,
And I will luve thee still, my dear,
Till a' the sea gang dry.

Till a' the sea gang dry
And the rocks melt wi' the sun!
And I will luve thee still, my dear,
While the sands o' life shall run.

And fare thee weel, my only luve,
And fare thee weel a while!
And I will come again, my luve,
Tho' it were ten thousand mile!

Robert Burns
(1759–1796)

RARE WILLY DROWNED IN YARROW

Willy's rare, and Willy's fair,
And Willy's wondrous bonny;
And Willy hecht to marry me
Gin e'er he married ony.

Yestreen I made my bed fu' braid,
This night I'll mak' it narrow;
For a' the live-lang winter nicht,
I'll lie twin'd of my marrow.

O came you by yon waterside,
Pu'd you the rose or lily?
Or came you by yon meadow green?
Or saw you my sweet Willy?

She sought him east, she sought him west,
She sought him braid and narrow;
Syne in the clifting of a craig
She found him drowned in Yarrow.

Anon

ROMANCE

I will make you brooches and toys for your delight
Of bird-song at morning and star-shine at night.
I will make a palace fit for you and me,
Of green days in forests and blue days at sea.

I will make my kitchen, and you shall keep your room,
Where white flows the river and bright blows the
      broom,
And you shall wash your linen and keep your body
      white
In rainfall at morning and dewfall at night.

And this shall be for music when no one else is near,
The fine song for singing, the rare song to hear!
That only I remember, that only admire,
Of the broad road that stretches and the roadside fire.

Robert Louis Stevenson
(1850–1894)

The Witch o' Fife

Hurray, hurray, the jade's away,
Like a rocket of air with her bandalet!
I'm up in the air on my bonnie grey mare,
But I see her yet, I see her yet.
I'll ring the skirts o' the gowden wain
Wi' curb an' bit, wi' curb an' bit:
An' catch the Bear by the frozen mane –
An' I see her yet, I see her yet.

Away, away, o'er mountain an' main,
To sing at the morning's rosy yett;
An' water my mare at its fountain clear –
But I see her yet, I see her yet.
Away, thou bonnie witch o' Fife,
On foam of the air to heave an' flit
An' little reck thou of a poet's life,
For he sees thee yet, he sees thee yet!

James Hogg
(1770–1835)

TWILIGHT ON TWEED

Three crests against the saffron sky
Beyond the purple plain,
The kind remembered melody
Of Tweed once more again.

Wan water from the Border hills,
Dear voices from the old years,
Thy distant music lulls and stills,
And moves to quiet tears.

A mist of memory brood and floats,
The Border waters flow,
The air is full of ballad notes,
Borne out of long ago.

Old songs that sung themselves to me,
Sweet through a boy's daydream,
While trout below the blossomed tree
Flashed in the golden stream.

Twilight, and Tweed, and Eildon Hill,
Fair, and too fair, you be;
You tell me that the voice is still,
That should have welcomed me

Andrew Lang
(1844–1912)

PROUD MAISIE

Proud Maisie is in the wood,
Walking so early;
Sweet Robin sits on the bush,
Singing so rarely.

"Tell me, thou bonnie bird,
When shall I marry me?"
"When six braw gentlemen
Kirkward shall carry ye."

"Who makes the bridal bed,
Birdie, say truly?"
"The grey-headed sexton
That delves the grave duly.

The glow-worm o'er grave and stone
Shall light thee steady;
The owl from the steeple sing:
'Welcome, proud lady!'"

Sir Walter Scott
(1771–1832)

SOWER'S SONG

Now hands to seedsheet, boys!
We step and we cast; old Time's on wing,
And would ye partake of Harvest's joys,
The corn must be sown in Spring.

Fall gently and still, good corn,
Lie warm in thy earthy bed;
And stand in yellow some morn,
For beast and man must be fed.

Now steady and sure again,
And measure of stroke and step we keep;
Thus up and thus down we cast our grain,
Sow well, and ye gladly reap.

Fall gently and still, good corn
Lie warm in thy earthy bed,
And stand in yellow some morn,
For beast and man must be fed.

Thomas Carlyle
(1795–1881)

To Leven Water

Pure stream, in whose transparent wave
My youthful limbs I wont to wave;
No torrents stain thy limpid source,
No rocks impede thy dimpling course
Devolving from thy parent lake
A charming maze thy waters make
By bowers of birch and groves of pine
And edges flower'd with eglantine.

Still on thy banks so gaily green
May numerous herds and flocks be seen,
And lasses chanting o'er the pale,
And shepherds piping in the dale,
And ancient faith that knows no guile,
And industry embrown'd with toil,
And hearts resolved and hands prepared
The blessings they enjoy to guard.

Tobias Smollett
(1721-1771)

A ROSEBUD BY MY EARLY WALK

A rosebud by my early walk,
Adown a corn-inclosed bauk,
Sae gently bent its thorny stalk,
All on a dewy morning.
Ere twice the shades o' dawn are fled,
In all its crimson glory spread,
And drooping rich the dewy head,
Its scents the early morning.

Within the bush her cover'd nest
A little linnet fondly prest;
The dew sat chilly on her breast,
Sae early in the morning.
She soon shall see her tender brood,
The pride, the pleasure o' the wood,
Amang the fresh green leaves bedew'd
Awake the early morning.

Robert Burns
(1759–1796)

THE HEATHER

If I were King of France, that noble fine land,
And the gold was elbow deep within my chests,
And my castles lay in scores along the wine-land
With towers as high as where the eagle nests;
If harpers sweet, and swordsmen stout and vaunting,
My history sang, my stainless tartan wore,
Was not my fortune poor with one thing wanting –
The heather at my door?

My galleys might be sailing every ocean,
Robbing the isles, and sacking hold and keep;
My chevaliers go prancing at my notion
To bring me back of cattle, horse and sheep;
Fond arms be round my neck, the young heart's tether,
And true love kisses all the night might fill,
But oh! mochree, if I had not the heather
Before me on the hill!

A hunter's fate is all I would be craving,
A shepherd's plaiding and a beggar's pay,
If I might earn them where the heather, waving,
Gives fragrance to the day.
The stars might see me, homeless one and weary,
Without a roof to fend me from the dew,
And still content, I'd find a bedding cheery
Where'er the heather grew.

Neil Munro
(1864–1930)

BONNIE KILMENY

(Extract)

Bonnie Kilmeny gaed up the glen,
But it wasna to meet Duneira's men,
Nor the rosy monk of the isle to see,
For Kilmeny was pure as pure could be.
It was only to hear the yorlin sing,
And pu' the cress-flower round the spring;
The scarlet hypp and the hindberrye,
And the nut that hung frae the hazel tree;
For Kilmeny was pure as pure could be.
But lang may her minny look ower the wa'
And lang may she seek i' the green-wood shaw;
Lang may the laird o' Duneira blame,
And lang, lang, greet or Kilmeny come hame!

When many a day had come and fled,
When grief grew calm, and hope was dead,
When mass for Kilmeny's soul had ben sung,
When the bedes-man had prayed, and the dead bell
    rung,
Late, late in a gloamin' when all was still,
When the fringe was red on the westlin' hill,
The wood was sere, the moon i' the wane,
The reek of the cot hung over the plain,
Like a little wee cloud in the world its lane;
When the ingle lowed wi' an eiry leme,
Late, late in the gloaming Kilmeny came hame!

James Hogg
(1770–1835)

FALSE LUVE!
AND HAE YE PLAYED ME THIS?

(*from David Herd's Scottish Songs, 1776*)

False luve! and hae ye played me this,
In simmer, 'mid the flowers?
I shall repay ye back again,
In the winter 'mid the showers.

But again, dear luve, and again, dear luve,
Will ye not turn again?
As ye look to ither women,
Sall I to ither men.

Anon

TWEED AND TILL

Tweed said to Till,
'What gars ye rin sae still?'
Till said to Tweed,
'Though ye rin wi' speed
And I rin slaw,
For ae man that ye droun,
I droun twa.'

Anon

THE LIGHTNING AND
THE THUNDER

The lightning and the thunder
They go and they come;
But the stars and the stillness
Are always at home.

George Macdonald
(1824–1905)

BEFORE THE SUMMER

When our men are marching lightly up and down,
When the pipes are playing through the little town,
I see a thin line swaying through wind and mud and
    rain
And the broken regiments come back to rest again.

Now the pipes are playing, now the drums are beat,
Now the strong battalions are marching up the street,
But the pipes will not be playing and the bayonets will
    not shine,
When the regiments I dream of come stumbling down
    the line.

Between the battered trenches their silent dead will lie
Quiet with grave eyes staring at the summer sky.
There is a mist upon them so that I cannot see
The faces of my friends that walk the little town with
    me.

Lest we see a worse thing than it is to die,
Live ourselves and see our friends cold beneath the sky,
God grant we too be lying there in wind and mud and
    rain
Before the broken regiments come stumbling back again.

E. A. Mackintosh
(1893–1916)

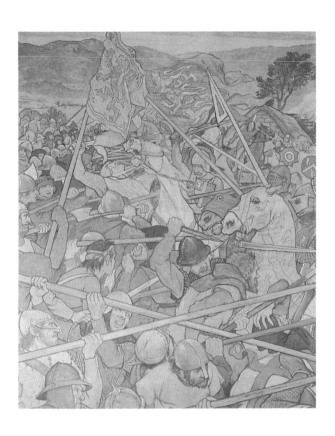

Scots, Wha Hae

Scots, wha hae wi' Wallace bled,
Scots, wham Bruce has often led,
Welcome to your gory bed
Or to victorie!

Now's the day, and now's the hour:
See the front o' battle lour,
See approach proud Edward's power –
Chains and slaverie!

Wha will be a traitor knave?
Wha wad fill a coward's grave?
Wha sae base as be a slave?
Let him turn, and flee!

Wha for Scotland's King and Law
Freedom's sword will strongly draw,
Freeman stand, and freeman fa',
Let him follow me!

By Oppression's woes and pains,
By your sons in servile chains,
We will drain our dearest veins,
But we shall be free!

Lay the proud usurpers low!
Tyrants fall with every foe!
Liberty's in every blow –
Let us do, or die!

Robert Burns
(1759–1796)

First published in 1992 by
The Appletree Press Ltd,
19—21 Alfred Street, Belfast BT2 8DL
Tel. +44 232 234074 Fax +44 232 246756
Copyright © 1992 The Appletree Press, Ltd.
Printed in Scotland. All rights reserved.
No part of this publication may be reproduced
or transmitted in any form or by means,
electronic or mechanical, photocopying,
recording or any information and retrieval
system, without permission in writing
from the copyright owner.

A Little Book of Scottish Verse

A catalogue record for this book is available
in The British Library.

ISBN: 0-86281-348-4

Acknowledgements are due to the following:
for all illustrations to the
National Gallery of Scotland.

9 8 7 6 5 4 3